TRADE THE PRICE ACTION

FOREX TRADING SYSTEM

By LAURENTIU DAMIR

TABLE OF CONTENTS

INTRODUCTION

First of all, let me just clarify one thing. The "50 pips" you see in the title on the book is to be taken as an average. It does not suggest or guaranty that you will make 50 pips per day, every day. You will make roughly 50 pips per day, on average. Some days you will make nothing, some days you will make way more than just 50 pips.

On average, at the end of the month, you will find that you have come close to this goal, that the following material tries to accomplish.

Before you start to construct your trading system, you must first think about what is the trading style that suits you better.

Do you want to sit in front of the computer the whole day entering and closing trades on the 5 minute time frame or do you think that trading on a higher time frame will suit you better?

My advice to you is very simple and clear: always seek to trade on the higher time frames. It is easier to trade this way and it will make you much more money in the long term. If you are a beginner in trading, it is best for you not to day trade until you gain experience.

Trading on small time frames carries high risk due to short-term random moves that are almost impossible to predict. Not to mention that trading this way makes you vulnerable against economic news events that come out multiple times per day and usually have a big impact on the small timeframes.

Even after you get more experienced by trading successfully on the higher time frames and you think you are ready to day trade, my advice is to not trade on any interval smaller than the 30 minutes.

Moreover, if you do decide to day trade, consider it as a backup trading style, day trade only when there are no trade setups as per your system on the higher time frames. Always seek to trade on the higher time frame. Nevertheless, as I said before, if you are a beginner trader, and you probably are, I strongly recommend that you develop your trading system around a higher time frame like the 4 hours or the daily.

Forget about day trading for a while. Build your trading system and trade on the 4h/daily charts until you start to add to your account consistently.

COMPONENTS

With the above in mind, the next thing you should decide is what you will include in your trading system from the technical point of view to help you win as many trades as possible. Decide what will be the core technical parts of your trading system.

From my experience, I can tell you which are the tools that work best in forex trading, with a great rate of success. These are price trends, support and resistance levels, Fibonacci ratios, price patterns and bar patterns/candlestick patterns.

These are the things you should consider including in your system. They are the most popular things in the forex market thus, they have the highest rate of success.

PRICE TRENDS

You surely know what a trend is. You see them on your charts every day. The trend is a core principle of the forex market or any market for that matter and should always be considered when constructing your trading system. It is always easier to trade with the trend than against it.

A trend signifies that the majority of traders decided to push the price in one direction.

You must always know what that direction is and trade in line with it.

If you want to know everything there is to know about forex trends, how to spot them by reading the price action, how to recognize when the trend is changing without the help of any technical indicators, you can check out the book Follow Price Action Trends that explains this in great detail, with many chart illustrations, and puts it together into a complete forex price action trading system that can yield thousands of pips by trading these changes in trend.

SUPPORT AND RESISTANCE

Support and resistance levels are also a key component of the forex market; a large number of traders out there highlight them on their charts and base their trading decisions on them.

Therefore, it is advisable that when you decide to construct your trading system you take them into account.

FIBONACCI RETRACEMENTS

Fibonacci ratios are another forex tool that works extremely well in the forex market.

Just pull up any chart and draw your Fibonacci levels from the start to the end of any big move in one direction or another.

You will see how many times these levels act as strong support and resistance zones where price bounces back to resume the previous trend.

PATTERNS

Price patterns and candlestick patterns are also very popular with the vast majority of traders therefore, they too have a great rate of success.

Price patterns are used as signals that price is preparing for a move in a direction and candlestick patterns are used mainly as a confirmation when entering a trade. If you want to learn in great detail about all of these above powerful trading tools and master them, you can take a look at the Trade the Price Action book that explains them very well with many chart illustrations and puts them together in the form of an extremely powerful price action trading system. In conclusion, these are the things that you should include in your trading system because there are by far the most successful tools to trade the forex market. It is completely up to you to decide if you combine them all in your system or just use some of them.

There will be more about these powerful tools in a later section where you will learn how to avoid making trading mistakes when working with them.

NO TECHNICAL INDICATORS

Now that you have an idea of what would be best to include in your trading system you also must know what not to include in it.

Do not use any technical indicators in your trading because they are worthless, they will lose you money overall. You might win a trade today using them but you will surely lose all that money back and more by the end of the week. You should consider yourself very lucky if during one month you manage to break even by trading with indicators.

All indicators are based on past price action, the macd, rsi, or stochastic are not leading indicators. They are only leading you to losses. Being constructed of past price action they are all lagging. By design they follow the past price action, therefore, even if the signals they give would be accurate they are useless because they come too late for you to capitalize on them.

Always remember one thing: price leads the indicator, not the other way around. Do not be fooled when you do a back test on your charts and you see that using an indicator or a trading system with indicators would have made you thousands of pips.

That is just a trick. Real time trading has nothing to do with back testing. When you put that indicator to work in real time, you will soon see that you are wasting your time and money.

Always remember that price tells the indicator what to do not vice versa. The ultimate indicator is and always will be the price action itself. You should focus only on reading and interpreting the price action movements and not overcomplicate your trading system with useless indicators.

200 EMA

From my experience, this moving average is the only indicator that is worth incorporating in your trading system. It is the most important moving average of them all, all retail and professional traders keep an eye on it therefore price tends to bounce when it touches it.

However, it is best to use it in your trading system as

guidance, as a confirmation of what price action tells you and not as a tool to base trading decisions on.

For example, if your system is designed for the 4h chart, you will want to read the price action on that chart to know what the trend is. After you do that and see that the current trend is up or down, you can then look at the 200 EMA on the same chart to confirm and enforce your price action reading.

 Let us say the price action trend on that chart is up. If that specific forex pair trades above the 200 EMA at that time on the same chart then you have a confirmation of your price action reading.

You can check out the Trade the Momentum book for a complete trading system that uses this moving average along with some other powerful concepts of trading to make 200 pips per week or more.

Let us see a chart with this moving average so you can

better understand how price reacts to it.

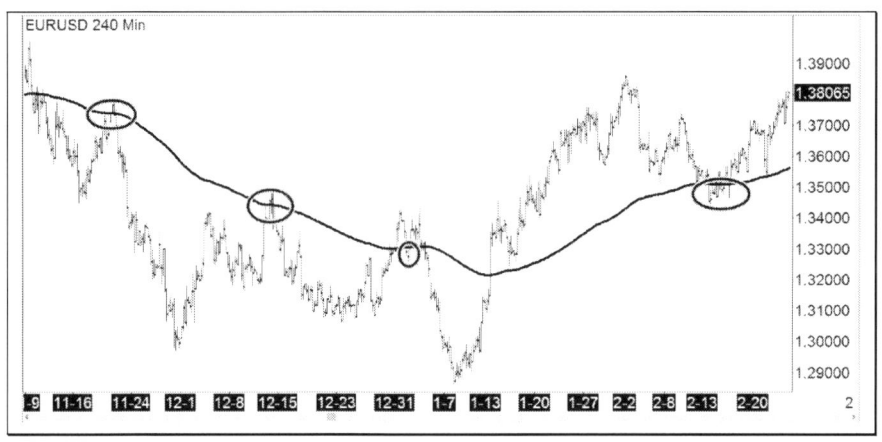

THE 4 HOURS AND DAILY TREND

A good trading system is the one that always refers to bigger picture. The bigger picture in forex is represented by the trends on the higher timeframes.

These trends control the price movement on the lower timeframes. If you design for yourself a system that trades on the 4h charts, you must always take into account the trend on the daily chart. If you trade on the 1h or 30minutes charts, you must always consider the trend on the 4h chart.

For the trend on the daily chart you can use the 200 EMA

discussed earlier. If the pair is trading above the 200EMA on the daily chart, it means that the trend is up on the daily chart. If the pair trades below the 200EMA on the daily chart, it means that the trend is down on the daily chart.

Therefore, any trades entered on the 4h chart according to your trading system should only be entered in line with the daily trend.

This is the way by which you can avoid severe losses and achieve long-term success. Let me show you a trade setup on the 4h chart generated by my Follow Price Action Trends trading system:

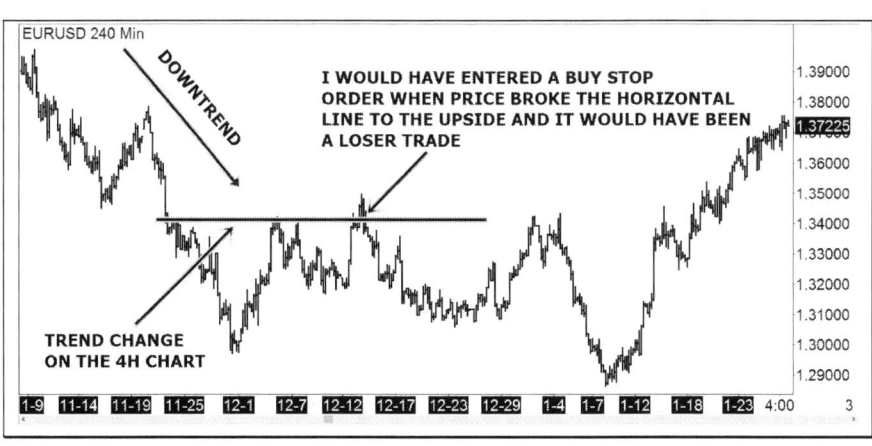

In the 4h chart above, a trade setup took place according to my trading system at that level where the trend changed from downtrend to uptrend on the 4h chart. I should have bought this pair at that circle in the chart.

Well, you can clearly see that price would have gone for a while in my favor only to retrace back down later eating all my gains and hitting my stop loss level. Is the trading system not good? The trading system is very good because it keeps me out of losing trades like this one. It always takes into account the daily trend. And the daily trend for that pair at that moment was:

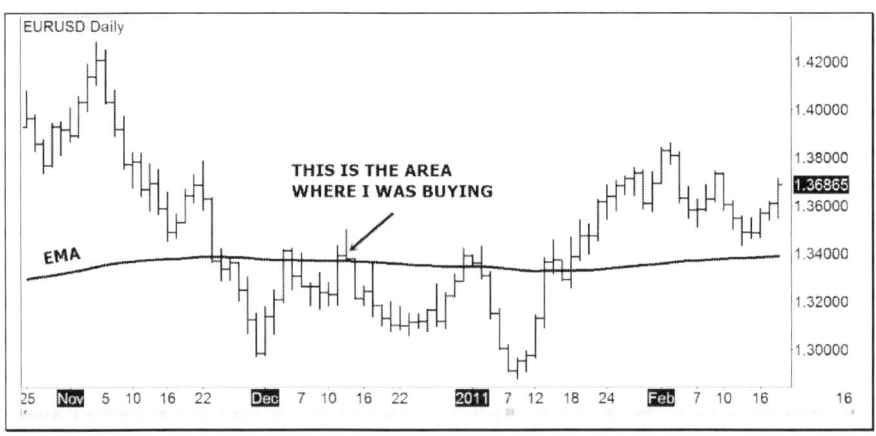

Well, the daily trend was clearly neutral at the moment when I was supposed to enter the buy order. The price action for that pair at that moment was below the 200EMA on the daily. You can see how price just touched the 200 EMA on the daily chart, creeped above it for a very short time period and bounced back down. As per my trading system, I would have taken this trade only if the pair had been trading above the 200EMA on the daily chart.

My trading system kept me out of this losing trade because it always looks at the bigger picture, yours should do the same. When you get more experienced and you want to start trading on a lower timeframe like the 1-hour or the 30 minutes the bigger picture in this case will always be the 4h trend. However, I do not recommend you to grasp the 4h timeframe trend just by looking at the 200 EMA.

The moving average works best to find the trend on the daily chart, for the trend on the 4h chart you will have to read the price action in order to get the best results possible out of your trading. You must determine the trend on the 4h chart by reading the price action, the moving average is not that correct on this timeframe and it can lead you to losses.

The smaller the timeframe, the less accurate the 200 EMA becomes.

The <u>Follow Price Action Trends</u> trading system teaches you with great detail how to spot price action trends on the 4h charts. In addition, the <u>Day Trading Forex with Price Patterns</u> trading system does a great job teaching how to correctly establish the price action trend on the 4h charts but with a different approach.

SOLID MONEY MANAGEMENT

The technical part of your system discussed earlier only solves half of the problem. The other half and equally important is represented by the money management component.

A very good money management technique gives you the opportunity to be extremely profitable with your system even if let us say, out of ten trades, five are losers.

Of course, if you build your system respecting all the rules above and the rules that will follow you won't be in this situation. If, for any reason you should find yourself in it, strict money management rules will make you profitable even in situations like this one.

POSITION SIZING

This is the first rule of money management.

For your system to be a good one, it must tell you how much money you are going to lose on a trade before you enter the trade in the market. To achieve this, you must first have a chat with yourself and think about what percentage of your equity you are willing to risk on a trade. My advice is do not risk more than 2-3% per trade.

Next, your trading system should give you the exact levels where you will enter the trade and where you will place the stop loss level before you enter the trade. Let us do the following exercise:

You have 1000$ in your trading account and you decided that you will only risk 2% of your money per one trade. This means that for the next trade you should risk losing only 20$.

Now, when a trade setup begins to take shape, you decide where you will enter the trade and where you will set the stop loss according to your trading system.

Let us say that you find out you will have a stop loss of 50 pips for this trade. This means that if the trade goes wrong and your stop loss is hit you should lose only 20$. You then divide 20$ / 50 pips to see the value in dollars for every pip that you lose. And that value is 0.4$.

This means that for every pip that goes against you towards your stop loss you should lose only 0.4$. Only after you have this value you determine your order size, which is a simple thing to do since now you know the pip value.

 This means you will have to trade with an order size of 0.04 lots (4000$). If you lose the trade: 50 pip stop loss multiplied by 0.4$ per pip equals 20$. You have to do this every time when preparing to enter a trade, always determine your order size this way, manage your risk, always put the bad scenario in front no matter how promising and rewarding the potential trade looks.

Don't you ever think about how much money you could win on that one trade. This will make you emotional, it will cloud your judgment, and you will be tempted to enter with a big order size to win more money out of the trade. Instead, always think of how much money you could lose and do the math explained earlier to determine the size of your order.

RISK-REWARD RATIO

Your system should spot trade setups where the reward is at least 2 times bigger than the risk for every trade.

This means that apart from the entry and stop loss levels, your trading system should tell you the take profit level also. You should know before entering the trade what is the risk and what is the reward.

If your system gives you trades where the reward is not 2 times greater than the risk or worse, the reward is smaller than the risk for every trade then it is not a good trading system.

You will lose your money in the long term. Whenever your system presents you a trade like this, do not take it, no matter how promising it looks. Let us do another exercise to see how easy it is to be profitable if you have a good system with solid money management rules: you have a system that gives you trades with 1:3 risk-reward ratio or more. This means that for every pip you risk losing, the reward is 3 times greater. If you enter a trade with 50 pips stop loss this means that your profit target is 150 pips.

Let us say that on a given month you made 15 trades according to your system, each of them with a 50 pips stop loss and 150 pips profit target. But, the market went crazy that month and out of those 15 trades only 5 of them were winners. 10 were losers.

Therefore, you have only managed a 33% success rates with your trading system, which is very low. Here is where money management shows its value.

Let us do the math. You lost 10 trades with 50 pips stop loss on each of them. This means you lost a total of 500 pips that month. You only won five trades.

With the profit target being 3 times greater than the risk, that is 150 pips won per every trade, this means you have won a total of 750 pips on that month. Therefore, you have lost 10 trades out of 15 which is dreadful but you've still made a profit of 250 pips on that month thanks to money management rules.

STOP LOSS PLACEMENT

Your stop loss should exist for every trade, but the stop loss must always be set at logical places in the market, not randomly. My advice to you is to always put your stop loss at the level where the price has very little chance to reach given the conditions of the market at that moment.

Let us see an example:

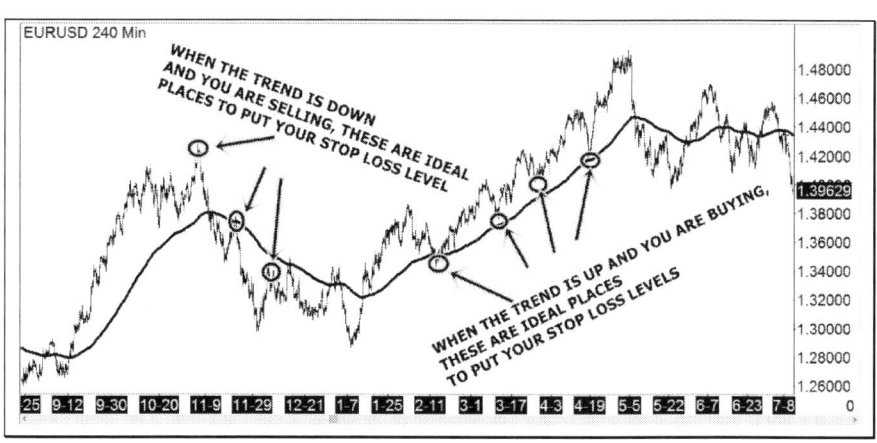

As you can see, when you sell, you put your stop loss just

above the swing highs that price makes. When you buy, you put your stop loss just below the swing lows that price makes on its way up.

If at the time your trading system gives you a potential trade you do not see a logical point in the market like these in the chart above, you do not enter the trade no matter how lucrative it might appear.

PATIENCE, NO EMOTIONS, NO OUTSIDE INFLUENCE

This does not have much to do with money management but it is very important and it has to be outlined. Without patience when trading in the forex market, you have only small chances of success.

If you construct yourself a trading system and 2 or 3 days go by without a trade setup you have to be patient, the setup will come, don't start to bend the rules and chase trades, there is no rule that says you have to trade every single day in order to make money.

Forex is about patiently waiting for the market to present

to you the perfect conditions for a winner trade.

Respect your trading system and trade only by its rules, the trades will come.

Do not be emotional when trading, leave your emotions at the door, and do exactly as the system tells you to do. If your system tells you that you have to trail manually the stop loss above every swing high but the trade has already gone 100 pips in your favor and did not make any swing high yet, wait.

Leave your stop loss at its original place; do not think emotionally, that you have to secure those 100 pips so you do not lose them. This makes you lose money. Completely disregard any comments from individuals on forex forums that tell you to buy or sell because they have the holy grail and they know better than you what is about to happen.

Only trade what your system tells you to trade, do not let yourself be influenced by anyone, no matter how convincing they sound. If you pay attention to some fellow that tells you to buy a specific pair, you will lose your clear and unbiased judgment and without even knowing, you will start to browse through the charts looking for trade setups that sustain that guy's theory and that have nothing to do with your trading system. It is your money; wouldn't you feel stupid if you would lose them by trading based on someone else's suggestions?

DON'T DO THIS

Now, after you finally construct your trading system according to all the rules above you must learn how to avoid making mistakes when putting your system to work.

PRICE PATTERN BREAKS

If your system includes trading price patterns, you must know that for a pattern to be considered broken price must close outside of it. If you have a trading system using price pattern breaks to signal your entry, then you must wait for a candle or bar to close outside the pattern on the same timeframe where you spotted the pattern.

Do not make the mistake to spot a pattern on the 4h chart

and then go the 15 minutes chart and wait for a 15 minutes candle to close outside and call this a break of the pattern. If the pattern resides on the 4h chart, you must always wait for a 4h candle to close outside with momentum, meaning that the candle should have at least half of its body outside the pattern to consider it a break. Let us see an example:

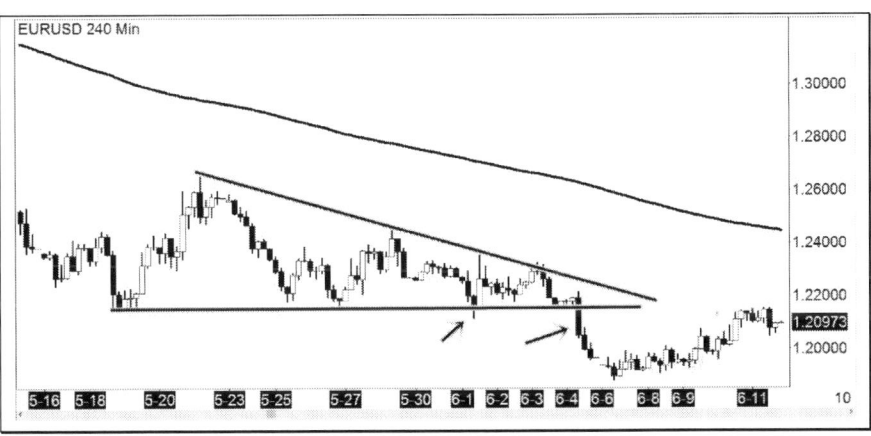

In the chart above, you have a descending triangle pattern. You can see that there is a candle that goes below the pattern but does not manage to close below the triangle at that first arrow there.

On the next candle, price quickly retraces back into the pattern. This is not a pattern break. On the second arrow there is indeed a candle closes strongly outside the pattern, with momentum; 3 quarters of its length are outside the pattern. This is a price pattern break. Even if the first candle that went outside the pattern would have closed at its low, that still would not have counted as a break because of the fact that it only went outside with less than half of its overall length.

If you are looking for a powerful trading system with price patterns and price action trends that can deliver more than 1000 pips per month you can check out my book Day Trading Forex with Price Patterns

CANDLESTICK CONFIRMATION

If your newly developed system uses candlestick patterns to confirm the trade entry you must always wait for that candlestick pattern to complete.

Wait for the last candle of the pattern to close before you enter the trade. If right at the close of the pattern there is some important economic news coming out they could invalidate your pattern and with it your entry signal. Remember that candlestick patterns work well because a lot of traders watch them and act on them. If you enter before the pattern completes and when the last candle finally closes you see that the pattern is not valid anymore then a lot of traders will not trade at that level because there is no valid pattern so you will be in the minority.

The minority always loses in forex. In addition, you have to know that candlestick patterns have their greatest success rate when found at price extremes. Let me show you what I mean:

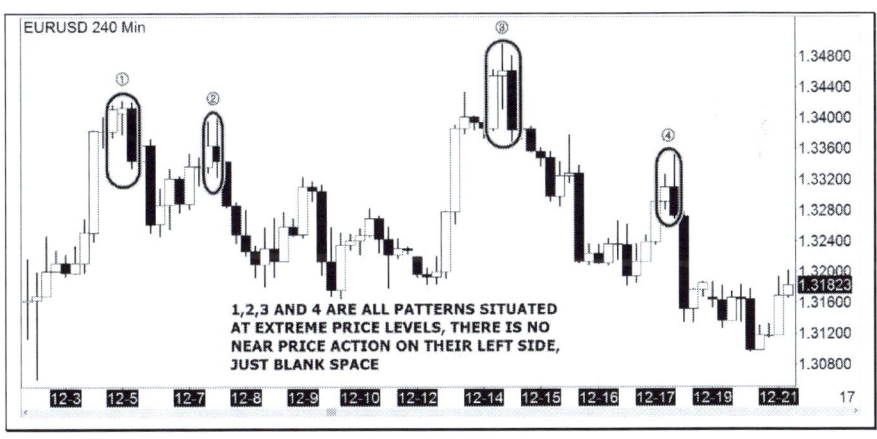

All the patterns in the chart above are situated at extremes of price. There is no recent price action at that level preceding them. These kinds of candlestick patterns have a very high rate of success. If your confirmation pattern takes place at a level where price action is trading sideways it might not be a very good confirmation signal.

FIBONACCI RETRACEMENT LEVELS

If you use Fibonacci levels in your trading system, then always wait for the price to touch the level you are watching before you consider entering a trade. Do not trade if the price comes close to your Fibonacci retracement level but does not touch it.

Let me show you what I mean:

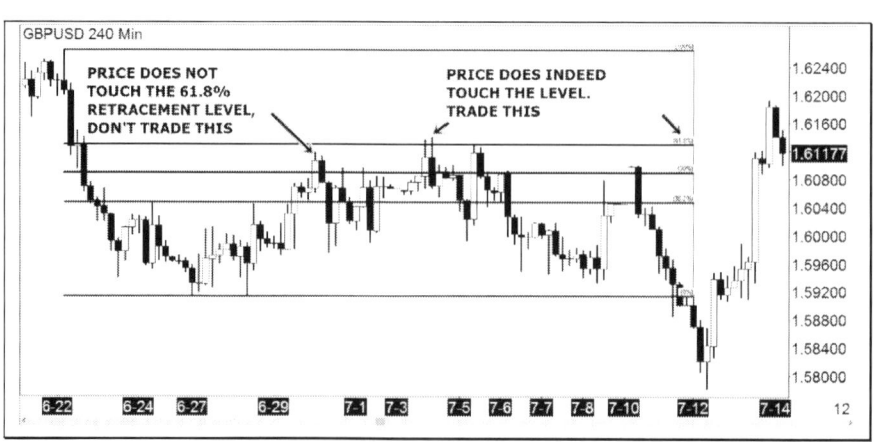

In the first attempt price comes close to the Fibonacci level but does not touch it.

It even makes a reversal candlestick pattern there suggesting that price will resume the trend down but soon after, price climbs back to the level this time touching and piercing it. This is the time to trade. If you had sold on the first attempt, you would have had your stop loss hit.

SUPPORT AND RESISTANCE

When trading with support and resistance levels make sure that you draw the most important ones, the pivotal ones where price bounces of them from either side.

These pivotal support and resistance zones are by far the most important ones they attract the most attention from the traders out there.

Do not beat yourself up with small, meaningless support and resistance zones. They are all over the place and they will clutter your charts for nothing.

Let me show you what a pivotal support or resistance zone

looks like:

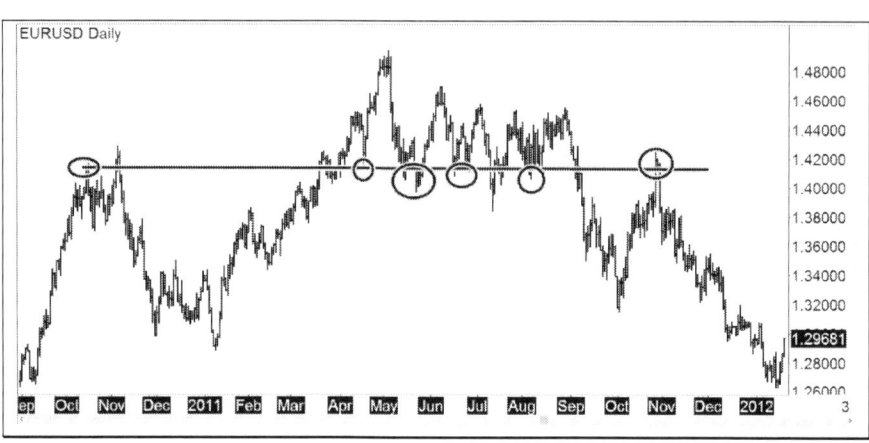

You can see here that price coming from the upside bounces 4 times off of the support shown by the horizontal line in the middle of the chart there, finally goes below it, and then starts to bounce off of it coming from below on that last circle on the right.

 The horizontal line is now acting as resistance after providing support for a long period of time, on multiple occasions.

These are very strong support and resistance zones that you always have to keep an eye on. They hold the test of time, when price comes towards them, either from above or below, it will react to it.

CUTTING PROFITS SHORT

This is a very common mistake made by novice traders. When a trade goes in your way for 100 pips do not close it in fear that price will come back to the entry level and eat all your profits.

Respect the trading system's rules and let the trade run until it hits your profit target or until it hits you stop loss level that you manually trailed above or below swings in the market.

You will never make money if you keep cutting your profits short because you fear of losing them. How would you feel if after you close the trade with 100 pips in profit, price goes on further and hits your target level at 200 pips in profit?

LETTING LOSSES RUN

This is also a very common mistake made by novice traders.

When you see that price is going towards your stop loss, don't ever move it further away thinking that it is just a spike in price and the trade will go your way eventually.

The second you remove that stop loss from its initial place decided by the system you constructed you put yourself under great risk.

Accept the small loss and wait patiently for the next trade setup. There will be some occasional loses; no system is perfect, just because you had a loss does not mean that you have to change the system because there is something wrong with it.

Accept the small drawdown and leave the stop loss level in its place otherwise, instead of a 20 pips loss, you will quickly find yourself in a position where you have no choice but to accept a much bigger loss.

It does not matter if you lose one trade, as you have seen earlier, you can be profitable even if you only win 33% of your trades with solid management rules.

REVENGE TRADING

If you lose one trade, keep calm, do not think to yourself that you have to recuperate the loss right away.

This is the worst thing you could do, to enter the market randomly and with a bigger order size, not obeying your trading system, thinking that you must get back the money you lost otherwise you won't sleep well through the night.

This is called revenge trading, and it clouds your judgment so hard that you could lose all your hard-earned money in a single day.

Close the computer and go about your business. Tomorrow is another day and you will get the money back surely if you trade according to your trading system.

50 PIPS A DAY FOREX STRATEGY
COMPONENTS

200 periods Exponential Moving Average

Support and Resistance levels

Candlesticks

This is a clean, easy to follow, and extremely profitable trading strategy to get you started in trading and to put you on the path of consistent profitability. It is better to trade with this strategy on the 4h chart but you can trade it on the daily as well.

 The bigger the time frame the more important it is for the overall market movements, therefore, the more profitable your trading will be. It is very easy to understand and to put in practice immediately, anyone can do it if they know the basics of how the forex market works, what a forex pair is, and how to open and close an order.

 I will now try to explain how each of the three components helps us to win trades with this strategy.

The moving average tells us what the main trend is on the 4h chart. This is very simple to do, just plot the 200 EMA on your 4h chart and observe where the current price is situated in respect to the moving average. If the pair at the current time trades above the moving average then the overall trend is up, if it trades below the moving average then the trend is down.

The moving average itself must have a clear slope in one direction. This means that for you to consider that the trend on the 4h chart is up the moving average must be sloping upwards and the pair has to be trading above it at that time. For a downtrend, the moving average must have a clear slope down and the pair has to trade below it.

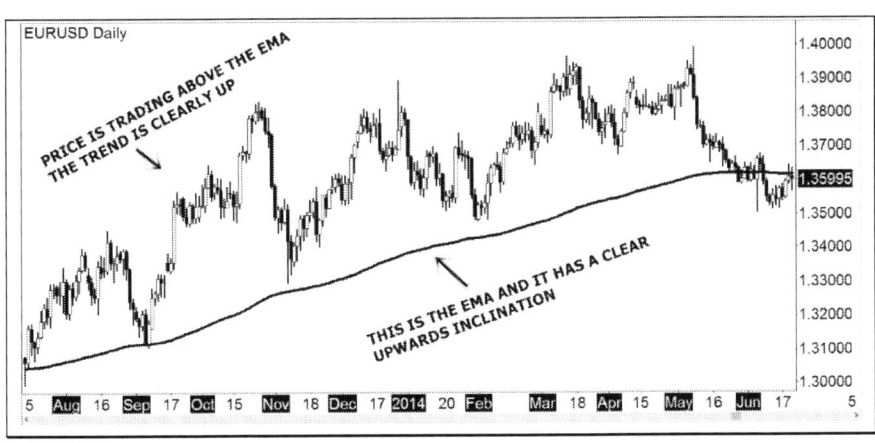

This diagram shows exactly how to spot an uptrend.

After we establish that there is a clear trend we then move on to the next level and we will try to find a support or resistance level.

I have told you that the moving average helps us to gauge the trend on a pair. If we find a trend, we go on further analyzing that pair to find a support or a resistance level, where it is most likely that whoever is in charge of that pair (the buyers or the sellers), will pick up the pace, and resume the trend.

The support/resistance level has to be a diagonal one and the trend line drawn on the chart to construct it has to be sloping against the trend.

You draw this trend line on your chart by connecting at least two distinct points in the market although three points will be better. Here is what I mean:

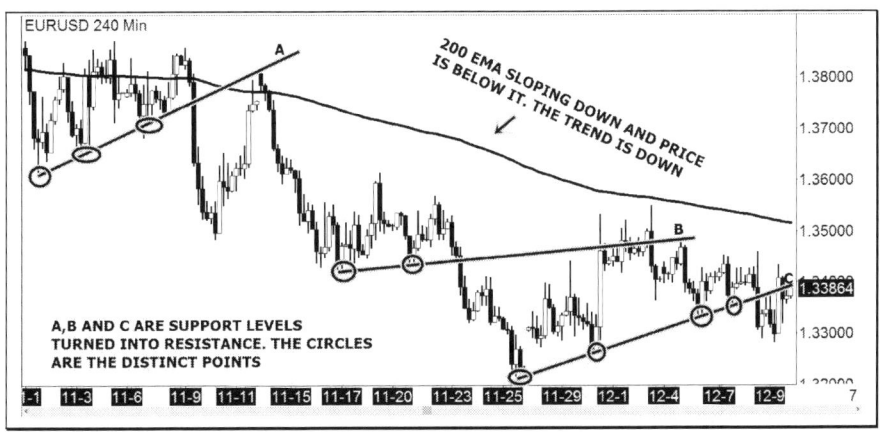

In this diagram, you can see that after recognizing a clear downtrend we move forward to discover three resistance levels one after another.

On the first one (A) we draw a trend line to connect the three distinct swing lows found there, on the second one we have only two distinct points, and on the third one, we have four points to connect with a trend line.

The more points there are to connect the better, the more important the support/resistance is. You can also see that all these three levels are pointing up against the main trend, which is a requirement for this trading strategy.

These three levels at first served as support for price action but once they were broken to the downside, they turned into resistance levels.

Now, about the third component of this strategy.

This strategy uses candlesticks to enter trades. After finding a clear trend and a support or resistance zone, you have to wait for price to go back to that support/resistance level and retest it.

This is where the candlesticks come into play. Before you enter a trade in the direction of the main trend, there has to be a candlestick confirmation that the trend is indeed resuming.

You will be looking for big body candlesticks that close at or near the high or low, which shows that there is momentum in the market and the dominant side (buyers or sellers) have decided to step in and continue the trend.

Let me show you the same chart above again to see what I mean by retest of the resistance level:

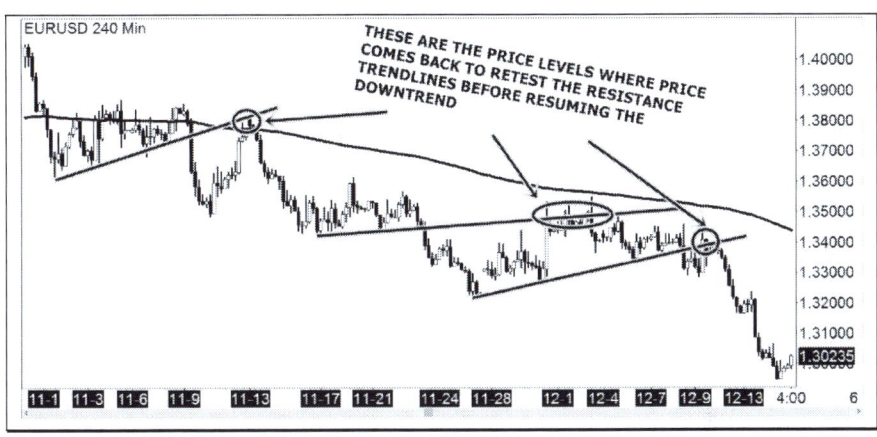

You can see that each time the support was broken to the downside, it turned into resistance as price gets back up to retest/touch the trend line previously drawn. It will not always touch the trend line like in the examples above; sometimes it will get near it and then resume the trend without a touch.

This is also a retest. In the diagram above where we have a clear downtrend and resistance levels in place, we also have now retest movements. After this point we will be looking for big bearish candlesticks with big bodies and with no/small wick at the close to signify that the sellers have entered into the market again to push the price further down and extend the trend.

Let us look at the same chart again but this time focusing

on what happens after the retest.

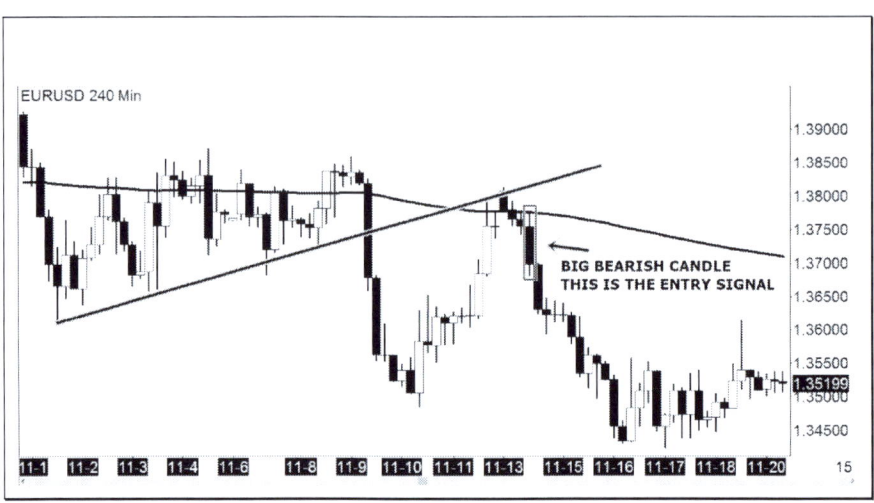

This is the first resistance level out of those three. There is a touch of the resistance trend line made by that big bullish hollow/white candle. After this price makes 4 very small candles that tell us this level of price is a key level where buyers have a very hard time trying to push the price further up.

This type of candles represents indecision in the market, represents equilibrium. From the beginning of the retest, buyers had no problem pushing the price up which you can clearly see by those big consecutive bullish white candles. When price got to the resistance level, the situation changed. As the main trend was down, sellers were in control of this pair and they were just waiting for a more advantageous level to sell again and resume the downtrend. These advantageous levels are always situated at a support or resistance level. It can be horizontal support/resistance, it can be diagonal like the ones we are discussing, it can be a Fibonacci retracement level, which also acts as support and resistance, it can be the 200 period moving average on the daily chart or it can be a combination of some or all of the above.

The important thing to remember is that these are logical points in the market where buyers or sellers are most likely to step in and resume the main trend.

Okay, after those 4 small candles that tell us the buyers are losing their power, comes a big black bearish candle, much bigger than the preceding 4. This candle has a big body compared to the preceding candles and also closes near its low.

This candle is the footprint of the sellers coming into the market to push the price back down and resume the trend. The close of this candle is the level where you would have to sell this pair. When looking after big candles to enter the market after a retest of support/resistance it is important to always compare that candle with the preceding 2-3-4 candles. The entry candle always has to be bigger than the preceding ones, has to have a big body and close at or near the low if it is bearish or at or near its high if it is a bullish big candle that signifies the uptrend will resume.

You might think that I am exaggerating the importance of this entry candle. Well, to help you realize what it really means and why I say it is the footprint of the sellers coming into the market (in this downtrend example) you must think of these 4h candles from a time perspective. Before this big black candle in the example above there were three very small 4h candles that did not push the price up or down, it just traded there in a very small range.

When the big candle emerges, we see that the price pushed down and away from that small range. This signal candle is bigger than all of the preceding three combined and it was formed in 4 hours. The last three took 12 hours to form. This is what shows us the sellers have entered the market. In only 4 hours, they managed to move the price down more than they did in the last 12 hours. Let us see the second example:

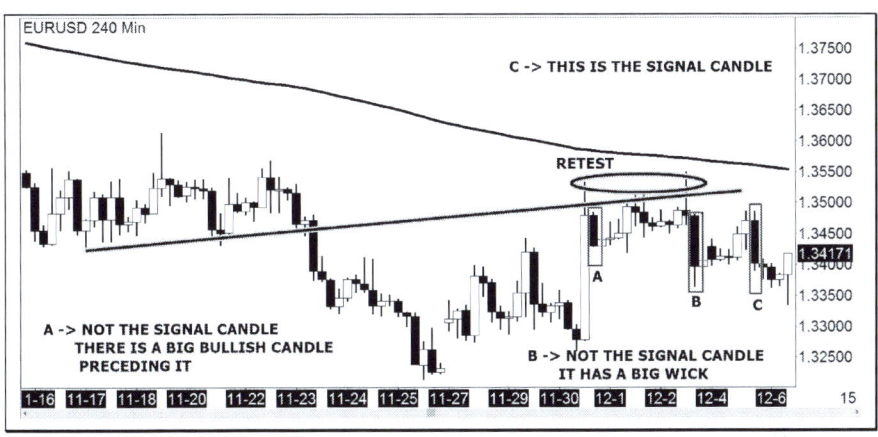

In this second example, you can see that after the retest of the resistance trend line there are three bearish candles with decent body size, which would imply that sellers have stepped into the market again.

However, the first candle (A) of these three is preceded by a huge bullish white candle. This is not our signal to sell.

The second one(B) is bigger than the first and also has no big candles preceding it. However, you can see that it does not close at or near its low, it has a big wick there, price has retraced from the low of this candle and closed almost at its middle.

This does not give us the momentum we want when entering a trade. Finally, the third candle meets our requirements; therefore, we enter the short trade at the close of this candle.

This third example is a very interesting one because it brings up an important point about retest movements of support and resistance levels.

You see here that after price breaks the trend line to the downside, it comes back up very quickly to retest it, a trend line that has now turned into resistance, and then it makes a bearish black candle that could mean sellers have entered the market.

However, this is the 4h chart, this resistance line holds great significance, it took quite some time to develop, and a lot of 4h candles, the retest absolutely has to be bigger than two 4h candles. This is why you would have to disregard that first black candle as a signal to sell. It comes way too early; the retest has to be bigger two candles. If this would have been the 5 minutes or the 15 minutes chart, and the resistance level developed in 3 hours or so then yes, the retest could have been composed of just two candles.

Still, this is a very important resistance on the 4h chart that took days to develop; the retest will more than likely be bigger than two candles.

After this black candle, we see that there are additional candles that just stagnate around that area completing the retest of the resistance level.

Finally, we have a valid signal candle that indeed pushes the price way down(B).

STOP LOSS MANAGEMENT AND TAKE PROFIT LEVELS

Now that you know how and when to enter a trade let us discuss about where to set your stop loss levels, how to trail them manually, and how to determine your ideal take profit levels. The initial stop loss level that you set when entering the trade has to always be set at above or below the level where the retest of the support/resistance ends. After this, when price goes in your favor you trail manually your stop loss above or below every swing/turning point/minor support or resistance price makes. In addition to this, you will also be determining your take profit level before you actually enter into the trade.

This is very important from the money management perspective because there will be some rare occasions when after calculating your take profit and stop loss level before entering the trade you will find that the risk you will be taking with that trade is greater than the potential reward.

Otherwise said, you would have to risk losing more pips than you could potentially win with that particular trade. The risk-reward ratio in this case is not a satisfactory one.

When you find trades like this...DO NOT TRADE. Wait for the next opportunity. Money management makes you profitable in the long run; always keep this in mind. Be very disciplined when analyzing charts and entering trades.

Always treat trading as a business and not as a game. Let us see an example of how to manage the stop loss and take profit levels.

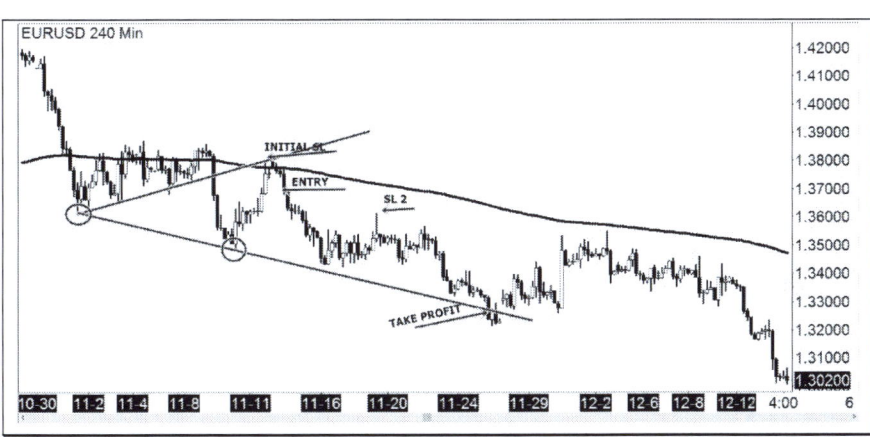

This is that first resistance level we talked about. Before entering the trade at the close of the signal black candle, you predetermine your take profit level in the following way: join with a trend line two points, the first swing of the resistance trend line and the point where the retest movement started.

The first swing of the resistance is the upper circle in this chart and the start of the retest is the second circle.

After this, extend this trend line down, and where the future price action will touch it, that is your take profit and the level where you exit the trade.

The stop loss will be set initially where the retest finished like shown in this chart and after this, as price progresses down it gives you logical turning points in the market where you can trail the stop loss (SL2).

Also in this example, you can see before entering the trade that the risk is far less than the reward. This was a 420 pips winning trade.

In this second example, the trend line for the take profit level extends far out of reach for the current price but, as long as the reward is greater than the risk(and it is), you will have no problem in entering the trade and trailing your stop loss above every turning point until it finally gets hit.

This trade actually went more in favor than this chart can illustrate and managed 550 pips of profit.

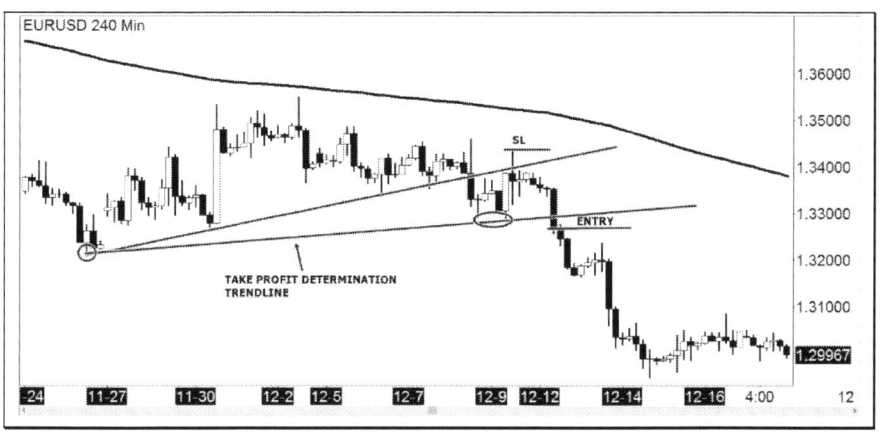

This is the example with that small retest. Before entering the trade, you draw the trend line to find out where your potential take profit will be and you see that you would have to exit the trade before you even enter it which is of course non-sense.

In addition, if that trend line would have been 10 pips lower and you would have had the chance to enter the trade, this was still not a good trade because the risk would have been greater than the 10 pips reward. Stay out of trades like this one.

There will be plenty of opportunities, this kind of trades happen frequently. An alternative way to predetermine your take profit level when the first method renders the trade unsatisfactory because of the high risk and low reward is the following:

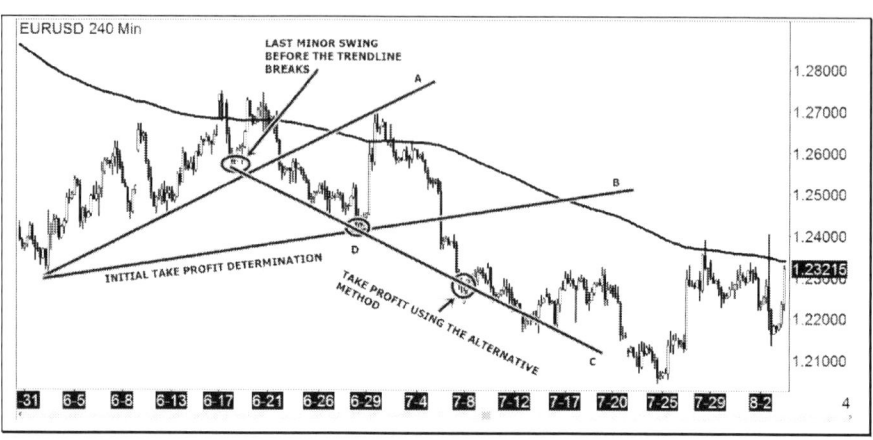

Connect with a trend line the last minor swing the pair made before the trend line(A) was broken to the downside (in the case of a downtrend) and the same start of the retest move(D circle).

Use whichever method gives you a better take profit level as long as it is not exaggerated and you think there are extremely low chances that the market will actually go to that level. If this method also does not help you achieve a good risk-reward ratio, then ignore the trade completely.

A second method that you can use to take advantage of the fact that every support becomes a resistance and every resistance becomes a support level after they have been broken it to use the same rules as with the method above, but applying them to horizontal support and resistance zones this time. However, with the diagonal support and resistance zones you have seen that they are formed by connecting two or more distinct swings in the market. With the horizontal levels, often times, you will not have a second distinct swing that you can use to draw a horizontal line. Knowing this, you must leave the candlestick chart and go to the same 4-hours chart, but a bar chart this time, and zoom it out completely.

Let me show you an example of this.

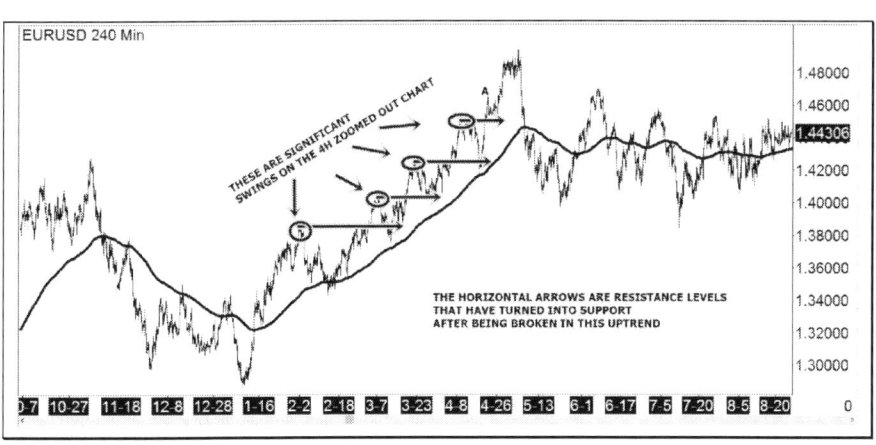

Please note that these horizontal levels come into existence just by drawing an extended horizontal line at the level where the important swings in the market are. If you want to trade the retest of these levels successfully, you have to make sure initially that they hold great importance to the overall movements of your particular forex pair. A way to make sure of this is by zooming out completely the chart like in the example above to see the big picture of the price action movements.

This way, you can put your support or resistance level into context, you can judge by looking at the surrounding price action if a swing is indeed important or not.

For example, in the chart above, after the last horizontal level, there is a minor swing that price has made there(A). You can see that I have not considered it as I think that this swing is smaller than the preceding ones on this pair and it does not hold great significance to the overall context of this pair.

Size of the swings matters. The small one is important on a lower timeframe, not on the 4 hours.

After you identify these meaningful horizontal levels, you will have no problem trading a retest of them, exactly like in the method above with the diagonal support and resistance areas. Let us see an example:

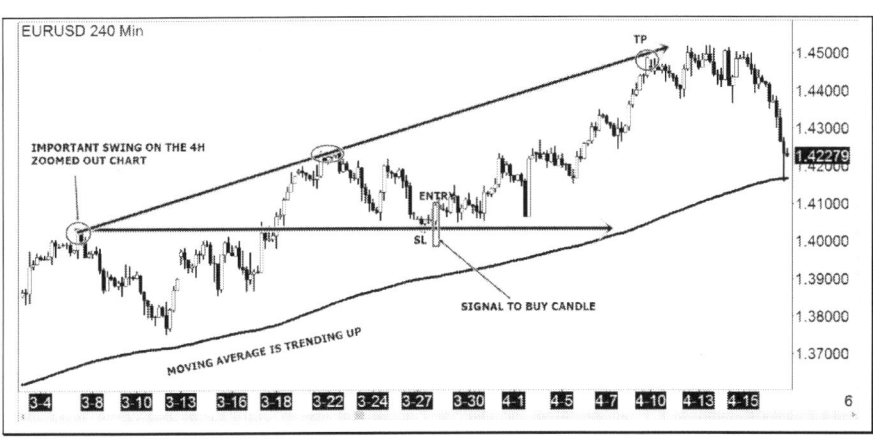

As you can see, things are clear in this trade example. The moving average is sloping up and the pair is trading above it. There is a clear uptrend.

You zoom out the chart and you find that this swing is actually quite significant by looking at the big picture.

You draw the extended horizontal line and you go back to the candlestick zoomed in chart to wait for the retest to take place(which is what this chart is showing).

The retest does indeed happen right at the horizontal support level and soon enough, you have a confirmation that the buyers have entered into the market again at this level and they are most likely to push the price upwards and extend the uptrend.

The confirmation is represented by that big, white, bullish candle that is also your signal candle to enter a buy order. The buy order is opened at the close of the signal candle of course. Trade management (stop loss and take profit) is made exactly like with the diagonal levels method.

In the end I would like to apologize if I sound a little rigid in my explanations and if there are any misspellings. English is not my first language. I am doing the best I can.

If you find that this adds value to your trading please consider writing a review of the book on Amazon. It does not have to be long, just a few words to state your opinion about the trading system presented in order to help other people make more informed decisions.

Thank you for reading this book and happy forex trading. Hope you found it valuable.

TRADE THE PRICE ACTION STRATEGY

TABLE OF CONTENTS

STRATEGY INTRODUCTION

I have been trading currencies with decent success so far and I decided to present to you my complete detailed trading system.

This strategy addresses people that have yet to succeed in the currency market, the people that have been trying hard to construct a winning strategy that will allow them to make some profits in the forex market.

I know this process is very frustrating but you have come to the right place. I've put together this powerfull strategy for myself after about one and a half years of frustration when everything I tried did not seem to work for me at all.

After all that screen time, studying the charts endlessly, reading countless books, articles, forums, I have come to the conclusion that the most powerful things, the things that work best in the foreign exchange market are the following: trend, support and resistance zones (both horizontal and diagonal), Fibonacci ratios and candlestick patterns/price patterns.

Consequently, I came up with this price action strategy that incorporates all of the above, and since then, things have been working out great for me.

NO INDICATORS

As this is a strategy based on price action, it doesn't use technical indicators.

As far as I am concerned all indicators are lagging behind the price because of the simple fact that they are constructed with past price information.

This makes them useless in predicting future price movements. The price action itself is the best indicator that you can have to help you make a lot of winning trades in the foreign exchange market.

You just need to learn how to read it and this is exactly what you will find out with this strategy.

The only indicator that I find useful is the 200 period exponential moving average or 200EMA applied on the daily chart, but not because it has the ability to predict future price movements, after all, it is just like any other indicator based on past price action, but for the fact that a large majority of the traders out there seem to be keeping an eye on it to the point that it becomes self fulfilling.

If you look at a daily chart with the 200 EMA on it you will see that price very often reacts at or near this moving average which means that there are a lot of traders that take into account this 200EMA and base some of their trading decisions on it.

The exact same story is valid for the candlestick patterns. The strategy I made includes the 200 EMA inserted on the daily chart, but only for confirmation that it is in line with our price action reading, we do not base trading decisions on the moving average.

TIMEFRAME

The 4hours timeframe zoomed out to the maximum is the best timeframe to trade if you want to make money.

A smaller timeframe than the zoomed out 4h is intraday trading and it won't make a very successful trader out of you in the long term because of the many random price moves on the lower timeframes generated by the never ending economical news.

The zoomed out 4h chart gives you an overview of what is going on in the market, it tells you which is the dominant trend and how you can profit from it.

Trading on smaller timeframes is very risky and I do not recommend it. In this strategy I use the 4h timeframe, as it is a conservative strategy, it is designed to make you money in the long run, and you will find that it is extremely reliable.

This is not a get rich quick type of forex strategy, you will not be making trades all day long, every day of the week. Substantial profits are made with just a few trades per month.

Also, your live account platform from your broker has to have the New York closing time for their charts, if they don't, use a demo account from a broker that has this like Fxdd or Fxlite, do all the preparation work on that demo account and use the live account only to ente the trades into the market.

Now, I will walk through the components of the strategy I mentioned earlier and discuss them in detail.

TREND

This is the most important part of the strategy. I will explain how to identify the trend by looking at price action, which is the most reliable way to do it.

 As you probably know, you have a trend in place as the price starts to make higher highs (HH) and higher lows (HL) or lower highs (LH) and lower lows (LL).

 Here is an example of a downtrend:

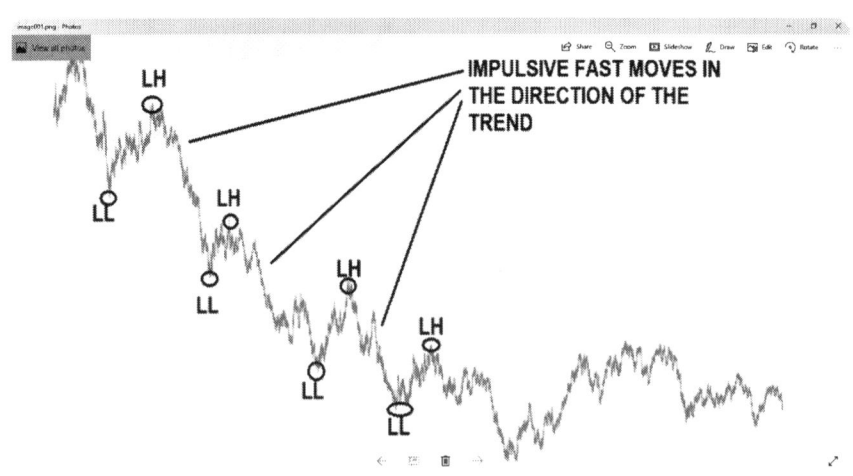

Now let's see an uptrend:

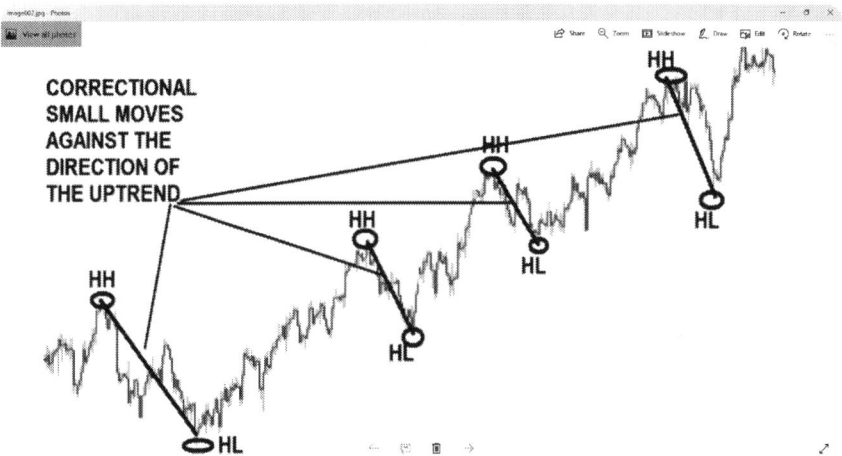

As you can see, when a trend is in place, price goes strong in one direction, than it corrects itself going in the opposite direction or just stalling/ranging for a period of time and after that, another impulsive move in the initial direction, another correction and so on. This is what constitutes a trend.

The important thing when identifying highs and lows is paying attention to see if they are of the same amplitude, like in the picture above for example. Here is what I mean:

In the same example after the third HH price made a very small move in the direction of the trend followed by a very small correctional move (the circles marked on the chart as smaller degree waves).

 That is not a HH as it is not of the same size or amplitude like the previous HH's. That is a small wave within the bigger wave.

One more example to illustrate this:

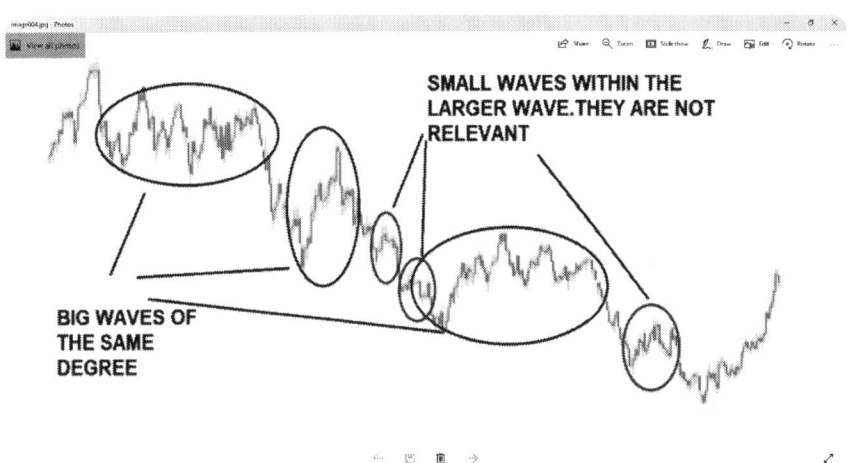

In this example you habe the same situation where there are small waves contained by the bigger wave.

This bigger wave is the one that has significance for the overall price action on this timeframe, those three minor waves are of a smaller degree and they should not be taken into account when deciding how to label your trend on this timeframe.

Okay, now that you have an idea about how to identify a trend, let's see how a trend changes its direction and identify that exact moment from a technical point of view.

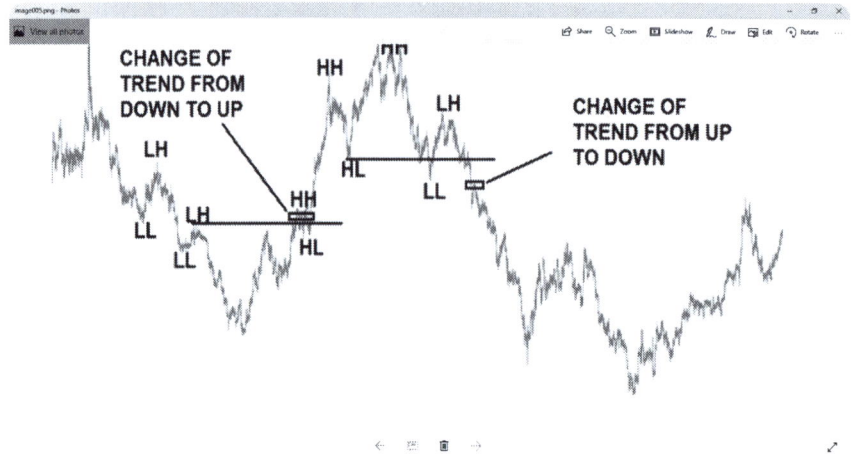

In the chart above you can see we have not one but two changes of trend. Starting from the left we see a clear downtrend with the price making LH and LL.

In order for the trend to change we have to see a breach of the last LH, right at that horizontal line. Until that happens the trend is still down.

You can see that eventually the price broke the last LH, made a small correction and then continued upwards changing the trend from a downtrend to an uptrend.

So, the trend changed when price stopped making LH, broke the last LH and made a distinct point in the market situated higher than the last lower high.

This point on the above chart is the first HH that price

makes after breaching the last LH of the downtrend. After this we can see another change in trend from uptrend to downtrend.

The price continues up and makes three HH's, but it cannot make a third HL as price, like in the first change of trend, breaches the last HL at the second horizontal line in this chart to make a new low at a price level which is lower than where the last HL of the uptrend is situated.

It then makes a correction move and goes straight down confirming that a LL has been formed and a change in trend has taken place.

Remember, a change in trend only takes place after the last LH or HL is breached, price makes a correction and shoots through the newly formed HH or LL confirming the validity of that new HH or LL.

Only at this time you know that the trend has changed. Here is another example to understand the importance of this:

In the example above we have a clear long term uptrend on AUD/USD.

Now, in order for this uptrend to be broken, price had to breach the last HL, retrace or correct and then go down past that point to confirm that the new LL has been formed and a change in trend has taken place.

As you can see, it did not do that, it only spiked bellow the last HL and then sharply retraced back up and never came down again to confirm the LL and the trend change. So the trend on the AUD/USD is still up.

OK, there is one more important thing that you have to know when you study the chart to see what is the trend. I told you already that a new high or new low has to be confirmed by price consistently going above or bellow it.

Let's take the same chart as the one above to explain better:

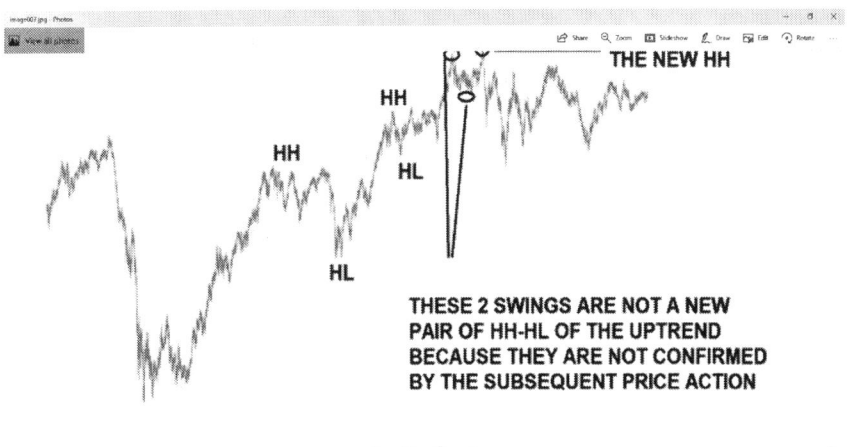

You can see that after the second HH, price made a consistent move above it , practically validating that it is indeed a HH.

 When price gets right at the top to that circled potential HH, it retraced and tried to move above past it to continue the uptrend and confirm the HH. It only managed to go 50 pips above it and then retraced sharply.

This was not at all a strong move above that level so the HH circled in the above chart was not confirmed.

The same applies to that new potential HL that could have been valid only if price would have gone strongly up. After this failure to confirm a potential HH and HL, the HH that remains valid is the one labelled „NEW HH" and the last low is still the second HL in the chart above.

All right, now you know how to spot a trend, with a little practice on your charts you will have no problem in identifying the correct trend and then try to profit from it.

Let's move on now to the other components of this strategy.

SUPPORT AND RESISTANCE

You probably already know that support and resistance are zones where price has reversed direction in the past.

For example all the highs and lows in the above charts are minor support and resistance zones.

Major support and resistance are those areas where price has repeatedly reversed direction.

The more times price touches a level of price and then reverses, the more stronger that support or resistance is.

There is also diagonal support-resistance or trend lines which work the same way as horizontal support-resistance.

The important thing to remember about support and resistance is that when you have a trend in place, a broken resistance turns into support and a broken support turns into resistance.

I will show some charts for better understanding:

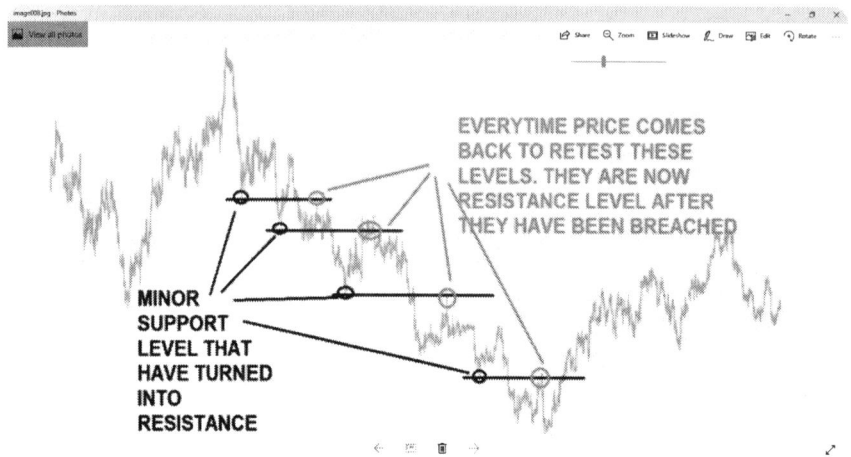

We have here a downtrend, all those lines are in fact lower lows that price broke to make new lower lows so they were minor support and after they have been broken they turned into minor resistance as you can see by the fact that after each of that zone was breached price came back up to retest it and every time it bounced back down.

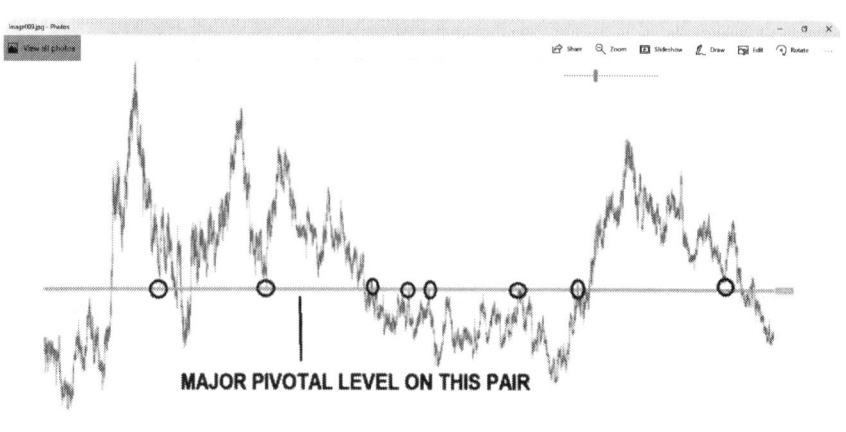

Here we have a major pivotal support turned resistance and then support again where price has reversed multiple times coming from both sides of it.

Here is another example of such a level.

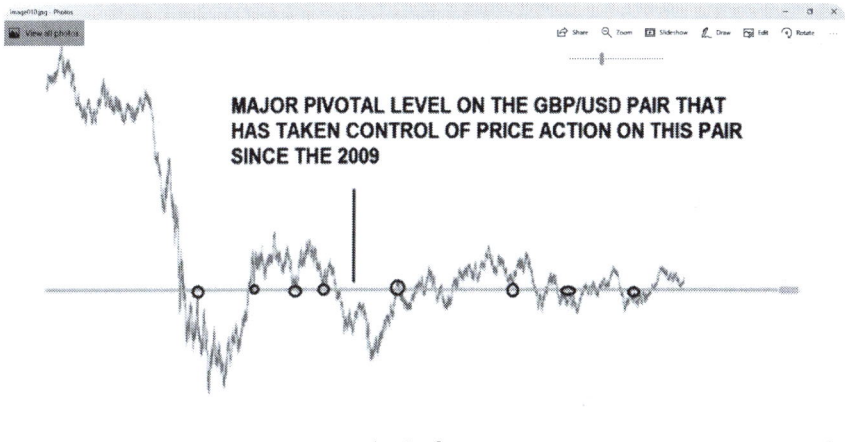

MAJOR PIVOTAL LEVEL ON THE GBP/USD PAIR THAT HAS TAKEN CONTROL OF PRICE ACTION ON THIS PAIR SINCE THE 2009

The important thing for you to remember about these powerful pivotal levels in the market is that they tend to attract price action.

The stronger the level is, the greater the chances are that price will revisit the level sooner rather than later.

Think of these levels as fair price or fair value for a forex pair.

When buyers or sellers feel that they do not have sufficient grounds to push the price strongly in one direction or another meaning that there isn't a strong trend, price will always go to revisit these strong pivotal zones in the market. They are like a magnet for price action.

Here we have a diagonal support or a trend line as it is more commonly known.

These diagonal levels are just as important as the horizontal ones but they do get broken faster. In this example you can see a trend line that was touched three times by price action.

In the majority of situations, when price comes back to the trend line for the forth time it will break it and cross below it.

Like horizontal support and resistance levels these too act as pivotal levels in the market as you can see in the illustration below.

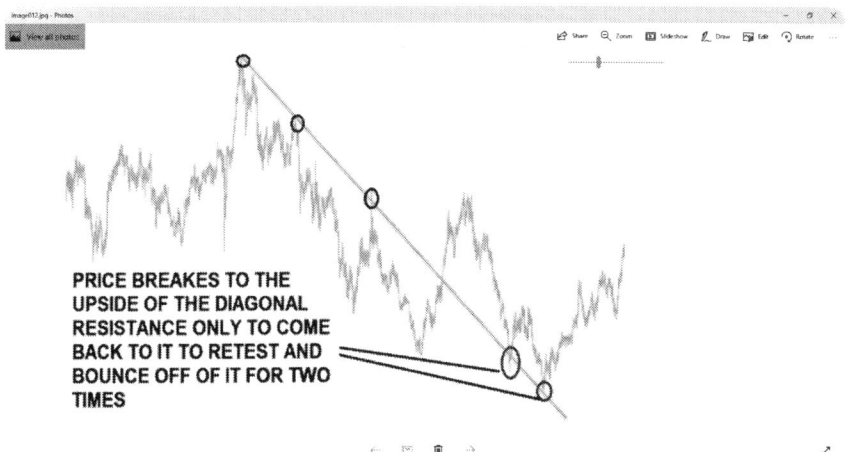

Okay, I think it is pretty clear now what support and resistance are. Let's move on.

FIBONACCI RETRACEMENTS

This is a tool that works great in the forex market. The vast majority of traders use it to find areas where to enter their trades.

In fact the Fibonacci retracements are just another form of support and resistance. Let's see some examples to find out how well they work:

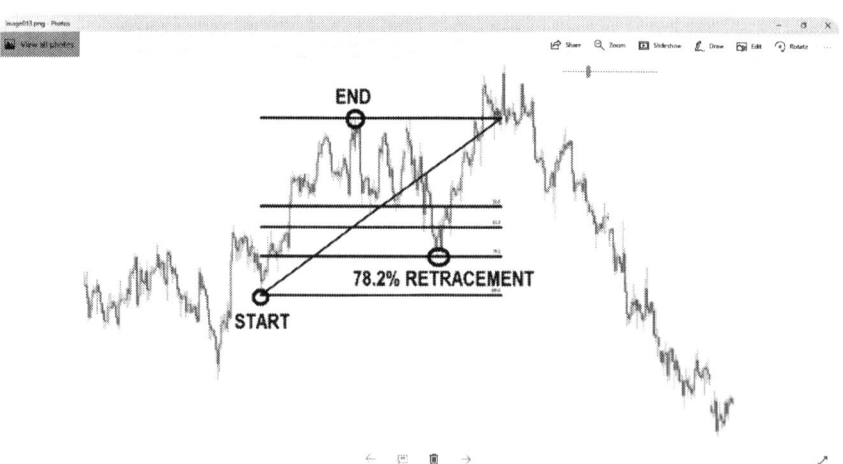

You can see, trend had just changed from down to up , price corrects itself exactly to the 78.2% retracement level and then rallies.

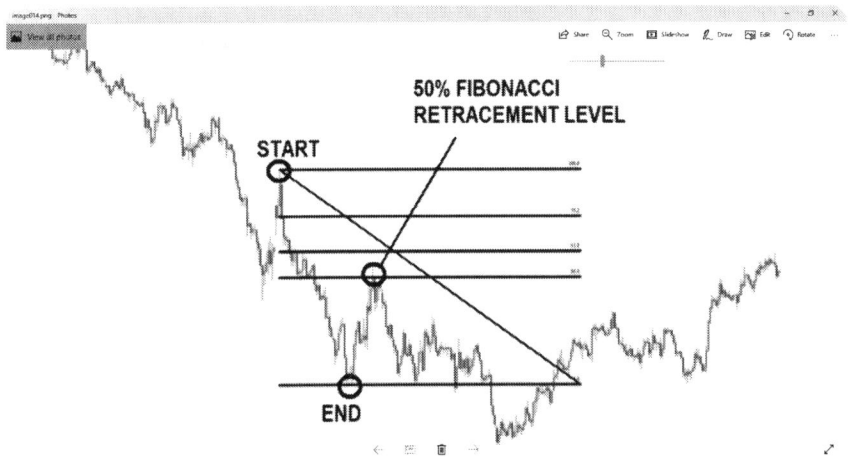

Downtrend, correction to the 50% retracement and then all the way down.

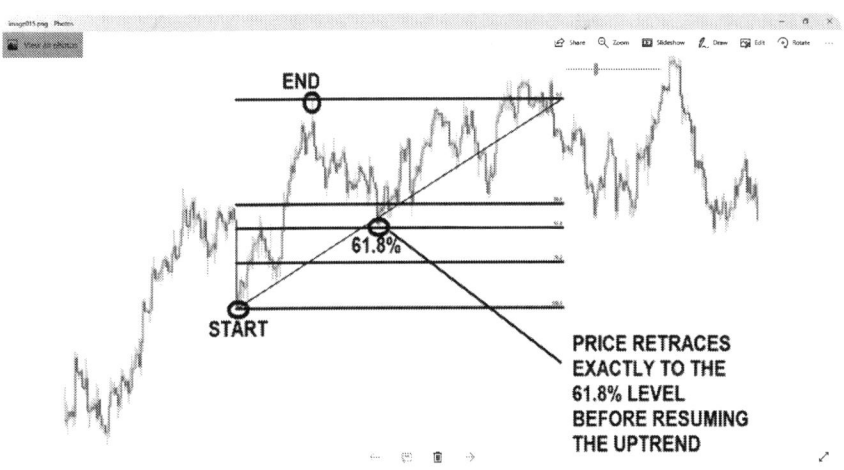

Uptrend, correction to the 61.8% retracement level and then rally.

From my experience , the 50% retracement is by far the

most reliable, followed by the 61.8% and the 78.2% in this order.

There is also the 38.2% retracement level but I don't use it because I don't think it is a complete correction, the price has to correct to 50% or more.

 There is of course the possibility that price retraces 100% of the previous move and it should be taken into account but the strongest level is by far the 50%.

 Also, an important aspect when plotting the fibonacci retracements on the chart is to see if there is confluence between a fibonacci level and a previous support/resistance zone like below:

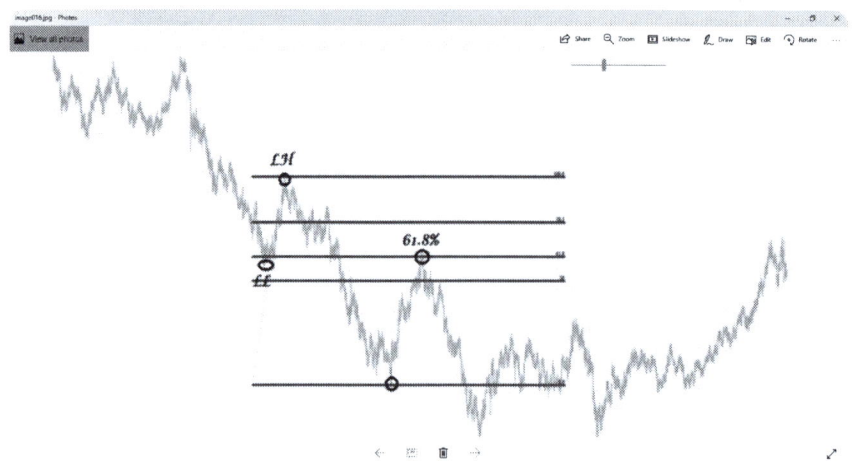

You can see in the chart above that the 61.8% retracement where the price reverses and resumes the downtrend coincides with minor resistance represented by the last lower low.

This is a stronger signal that the trend down will resume at this point because price has reached the 61.8% retracement level and at the same time that level coincides with a resistance zone.

If we have confluence of fibonacci retracement level with a trendline it is an even stronger indication.

If we have confluence of all three at the same level that is the strongest possible signal that the trend will resume.

Look at the chart above, we are in a very strong uptrend, we have a trendline in place, price comes back down and makes a correction to the 61.8% retracement level which coincides with the trendline.

This is a strong signal.

Furthermore, after that it comes back to the 50% retracement level which is also right at the trendline again and is also minor support represented by the last higher high.

This is a very strong signal. In conclusion, the more confluence of events at a specific price zone , the more stronger the indication that the trend will resume from that point on.

Ok, we now know in detail how to correctly identify a trend, we know about support/resistance zones and all about the Fibonacci retracement levels and how powerfull they are in conjunction with other support/resistance zones.

Let's move on to the last component of this strategy.

CANDLESTICK PATTERNS

As you probably know, candlestick patterns are used best as a confirmation when to enter a trade if a price action setup has been spotted.

I will give examples of candlestick patterns that from my experience are the most powerfull.

Hammer:

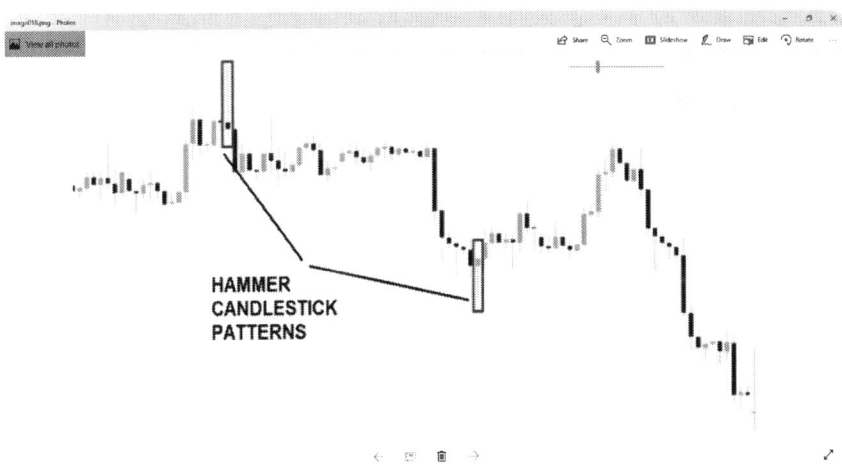

This is the most powerfull of them all. When this happens at an extreme like in the chart above, chances are price is going to reverse for a while.

And it did, even though the second hammer was a bullish one it still pushed the price up for more than 150 pips which is remarkable considering the trend was down at that time.

Engulfing pattern:

Very strong pattern. It means that a change in market sentiment has occurred.

As you can see it is at a price extreme which is what we will be looking for in this strategy when it comes to candlestick patterns.

When it forms at a price extreme the signal it gives is very powerfull.

Morning star/Evening star:

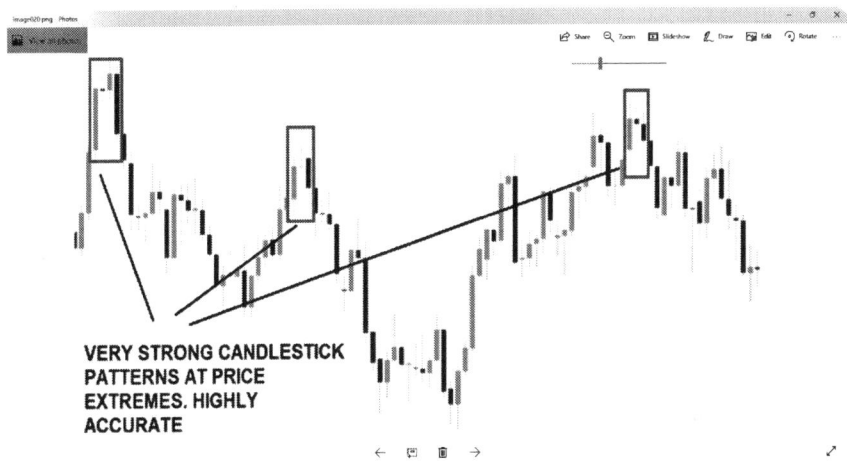

Very strong pattern as well as you can see at price extremes.

Strong candle in one direction, followed by one or more indecisive small candles and then a strong candle in the opposite direction that closes at least at the half of the first candle.

Dark cloud/ Piercing pattern:

Consists of a strong candle in one direction followed by a second candle that goes past the high or low of the first but can't continue further in that direction and closes way back in the other direction.

Other patterns that work just as well when found at a price extreme:

The first on the left has a first candle in a direction , the second tests within 1-2 pips the high or low of the first candle and then closes way above/below the first candle.

The second pattern on the right of the chart above consists of three candles.

The candle in the middle allways has the highest high , the first and third close way below the middle candle's low.

When two consecutive candles with roughly the same size occur at a price extreme it is a clear indication of a change in price direction.

Ok, now we know all about the components of this powerfull price action strategy, let's put them together and define clear entry/exit rules, clear stop loss and take profit levels so we can make some money.

STRATEGY STEP BY STEP

Move your charts to the 4hours timeframe zoomed out and insert the 200EMA on them. Remove everything else on the charts.

Identify the trend on the 4hours chart as we discussed earlier.

If there is a trend in place , go to the daily chart and see if the daily 200EMA confirms your identified trend, meaning that if you spotted an upward trend the price on the daily chart must be above the daily 200EMA.

If you have a downtrend then price must be below the 200EMA on the daily chart.

If things on the daily chart look the way they are supposed to and they confirm your new found trend then go back to the 4h chart and wait for a price correction move opposite to the trend direction.

When the correction move starts to unfold plot your fibonacci retracement levels on the chart and wait for price to get to the 50% level. If one of the candlestick patterns previously discussed forms at this level we enter a trade in the direction of the trend.

If no pattern occurs, we sit back and wait for price to go further to the 61.8% level and form a pattern. Same goes with the 78.2% level.

Chart examples to show entry / stop loss / take profit levels.

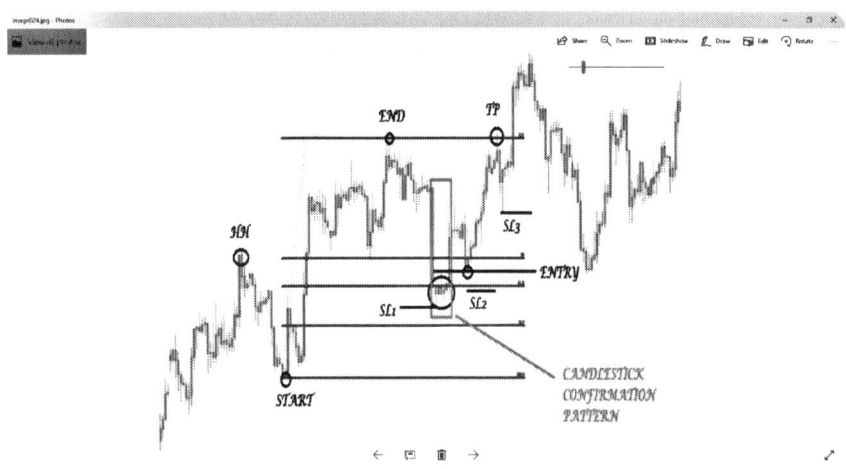

In the example above we have a clear uptrend , the daily chart confirmes it. We lay fibonacci retracements on the chart.

Price comes to the 61.8% retracement level and makes a

perfect morning star pattern. After the pattern is completed we know that there is a strong chance that the trend will resume upwards an we enter a pending buy limit order as pointed in the chart.

Notice that we find a logical place to enter the trade which is that small support that the candlestick pattern has formed.

The stop loss will allways be at the end of the pattern and the take profit level will allways be at that peak that price made before it started the correction move.

All the trades with this system will look just like this one with very low risk and high reward.

On this trade notice that risk is 30 pips and reward is more than 100 pips.

Important money management advice: if you ever find a trade setup where the risk will be greater than the reward do not trade it, no matter how good the price action setup looks like.

Also, the stop loss can be manually trailed bellow the minor higher lows price makes on his way back up to the top like shown in the above chart.

Things work just the same with all the other patterns as well.

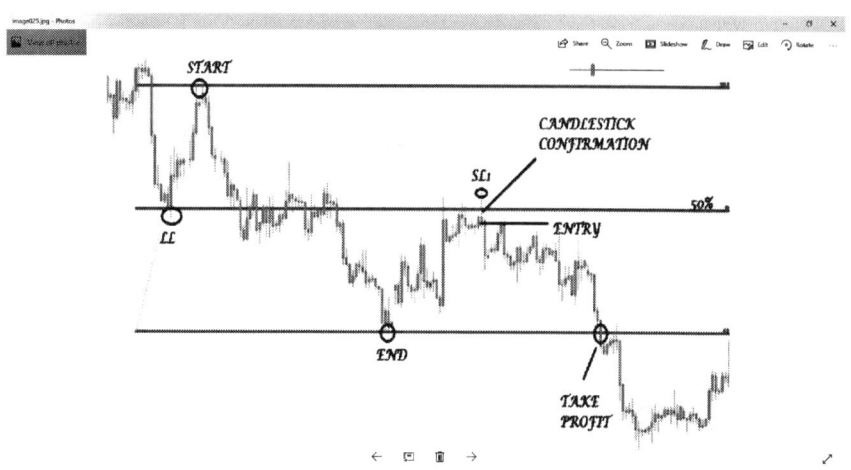

Another example, downtrend confirmed by daily chart, retracement back to 50% level, hammer pattern at that level.

We enter after the hammer closes, stop loss above the hammer, taka profit way down to where the retracement started.

You can see here that the 50% retracement also coincides with minor resistance formed at the last lower low.

As you can see we have a 75 pip risk and and a 265 pips

reward.

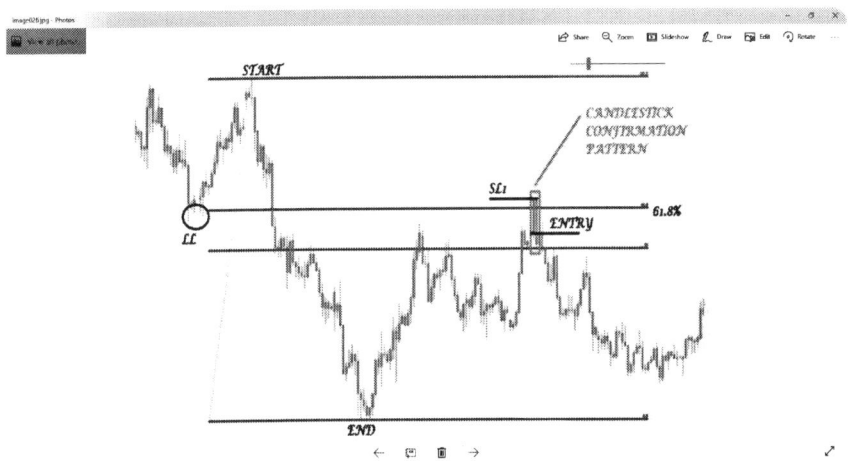

Here we have the EUR/USD pair in a downtrend, price is below the 200 EMA on the daily chart, the pair goes down strong and then retraces back up to the 61.8 retracement level where price makes a very powerfull candlestick reversal pattern.

A bullish strong candle followed by an even stronger bearish candle.

We can see that we have confluence of signals because that level is also where the last resistance represented by the LL is.

We enter the trade and put the stop loss in place like shown on the chart and let's see what happened next:

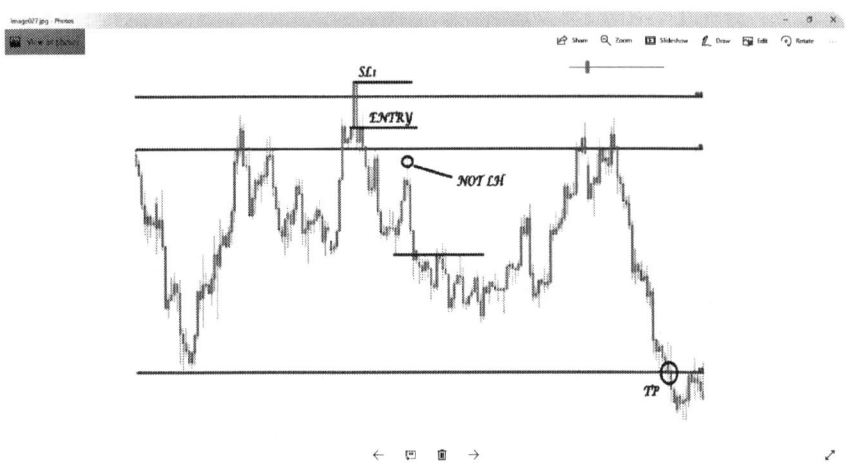

We see that price got eventually to where our take profit was situated,but it did not go straight down to it.

You remember we talked about trailing the stop loss only to logical places,which in this case would have been lower highs made by price on its way down to our take profit level.

Price did not make a lower high, it just traded in a range for some time before going strong down to the take profit.

That level circled on the chart is not a valid LH because it was not confirmed by subsequent price action.

Remember what we talked about earlier when we learned how to correctly identify a trend,any high or low has to be confirmed by price action.

In this case,after that potential circled LH, price did not go down with conviction past that minor support where the red line is, it was not an impulsive move to confirm the lower high.

Price just traded there in a range and after that it went up past that level and made a real lower low this time because it was later confirmed by price action going sharply all the way down to the take profit.

In conclusion,the stop loss should have stayed at its initial level and the reward was very big as you can see: 440 pips. The risk was only 90 pips.

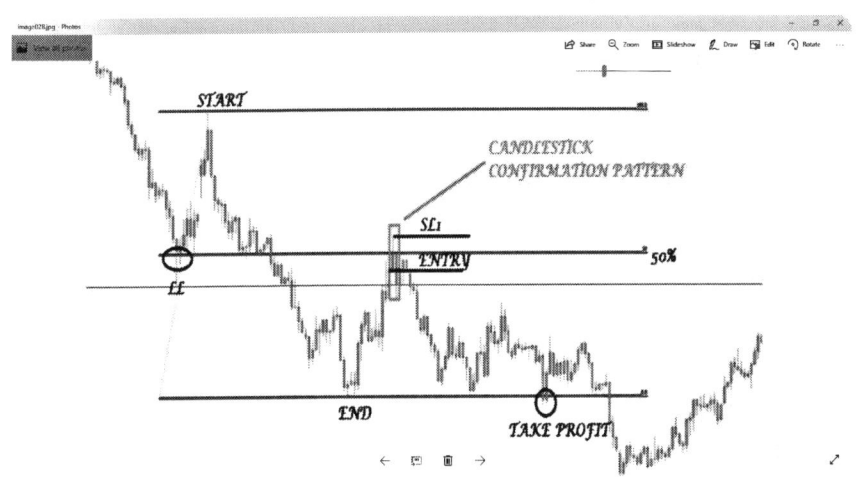

In this example, the same pair EUR/USD, strong downtrend confirmed by the daily chart,price retraces back to the 50% level which is also the last resistance made by that LL so we have strong confluence at this level.

 Price makes there a strong reversal pattern,we enter,set the stop loss and the take profit level and just sit back. Reward 420 pips / Risk 110 pips.

EUR/CHF pair,strong downtrend,retracement to the 50% level, price makes reversal pattern, we enter, trail manually the stop loss to that minor lower high(SL2) and we take 365 pips from this trade with a risk of 130 pips.

 Compared to the other trades above, the risk/reward ration on this is lower but it is still very good.

This example on GBP/JPY is very interesting. It shows you how important it is to respect the rules of this system, to wait for a candlestick pattern to form before you enter the trade.

Trend was up at that moment, price retraces back to the 50% level but it goes sharply below it.

There is no pattern here so we do not enter any trade, we wait. Price then goes to the 61.8% retracement level but no patterns is formed here either.

No trade here. We sit back and wait.

After a brief bounce, price comes back down again at the 61.8% level and finally, it makes the reversal patterns we have been waiting for.

 We enter the trade, trail the stop loss below that minor higher low(SL2) and we get 1400 pips with a 150 pips risk.

 But, to win those 1400 pips you have to be patient and wait for the price to get to the take profit, do not place the stop loss in random places closer to the current price thinking that it will not get hit, do not close the trade at half way thinking that 700 pips or so is enough,respect the rules.

This is how money are made, by holding on to winning trades not closing them at half way.

 Now, about the take profit levels, the safest thing is to take your profits and close the trade as shown above in all the diagrams, when price reaches the start of the correction move.

 Usually this level will get hit the vast majority of times therefore you will have no problem winning the amount of pips that you expected to win at the start of the trade.

 Another less conservative way that has the potential to bring you more pips per every trade but also can make you win a little less than what you would normally win by using the conservative method is to draw a trend line that connects the start of the correction move with the previous HH if in an uptrend or with the previous LL if in a downtrend.

After you draw this trend line, you extend it further down in a downtrend or further up in an uptrend.

You can then consider your take profit level, the point where future price action will touch your trendline. Let me show you a chart:

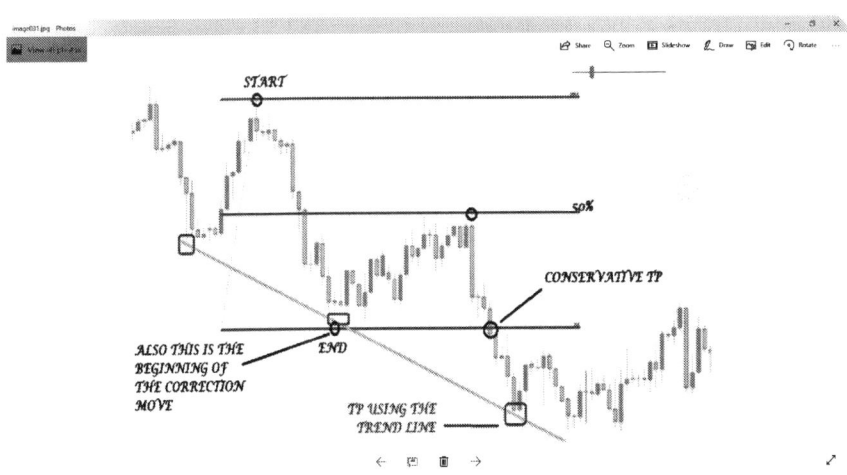

In this example above there is no trade because there isn't any candlestick confirmation pattern.

But if there were one, you would enter the trade and set your conservative TP at the start of the correction.

If you draw that red trend line like in the example you see that you can find a pretty accurate and more favorable for you take profit level because that line acts as a support for price.

Usually when there is a strong trend price goes beyond the start of the correction and touches that trend line but there are cases when the trend ends just at the start of the correction/conservative TP level or just passes that point for a moment and shortly after the trend ends and price reverses direction never touching the trend line.

This is entirely up to you, if you are more risk inclined go for the trend line option, you will not lose much if price doesn't get to touch it.

PATIENCE IS THE KEY

If you decide to use this strategy you will quickly find out that it is extremely powerfull and profitable you just need to follow the rules strictly and have patience.

You will not have trade setups every day you have to wait paciently for them to occur.

Do not chase trades, do not enter a trade if the requirements of this system are not fulfilled.

Wait for the patterns to completely form before you enter a trade.

Respect this system to the letter and you will make a lot of money trading forex as time passes.

This is it.

In the end I would like to apologize if I sound a little to rigid in my explanations and if there are any misspellings.

English is not my first language. I am doing the best I can.

Thank you and happy trading

If you find that this adds value to your trading please consider writing a review of the book on Amazon.

It does not have to be long, just a few words to state your opinion about the trading system presented in order to help other people make more informed decisions.

28191774R00059

Printed in Great Britain
by Amazon